We Need Transportation Workers

by Brienna Rossiter

FOCUS READERS®

PIONEER

www.focusreaders.com

Focus Readers is distributed by North Star Editions:
sales@northstareditions.com | 888-417-0195

Produced for Focus Readers by Red Line Editorial.

Photographs ©: Shutterstock Images, cover, 1, 4, 6 (top), 6 (bottom), 8, 11, 12, 15, 17, 18, 21

Library of Congress Cataloging-in-Publication Data
Names: Rossiter, Brienna, author.
Title: We need transportation workers / by Brienna Rossiter.
Description: Lake Elmo, MN : Focus Readers, [2022] | Series: Essential jobs | Includes
    index. | Audience: Grades 2-3
Identifiers: LCCN 2021042105 (print) | LCCN 2021042106 (ebook) | ISBN
    9781637390351 (hardcover) | ISBN 9781637390894 (paperback) | ISBN
    9781637391433 (ebook) | ISBN 9781637391969 (pdf)
Subjects: LCSH: Transport workers--Juvenile literature.
Classification: LCC HD8039.T7 R67 2022 (print) | LCC HD8039.T7 (ebook) | DDC
    388.092--dc23
LC record available at https://lccn.loc.gov/2021042105
LC ebook record available at https://lccn.loc.gov/2021042106

Printed in the United States of America
Mankato, MN
012022

About the Author

Brienna Rossiter is a writer and editor who lives in Minnesota.

Table of Contents

Chapter 1

Transportation

Vehicles carry people and **cargo** all over the world. Transportation workers make this possible. Some workers drive buses or trucks. Some fly airplanes. Others work on boats or trains.

Some people build or fix vehicles. Other people work on roads, tunnels, and bridges. Still others make deliveries. They bring people food, packages, or mail.

Fun Fact

There are 4 million miles (6.4 million km) of roads in the United States.

Chapter 2

Carrying Cargo

Trucks carry all kinds of cargo. So do trains. Workers load and drive these vehicles. Workers also help plan their **routes**. Other workers build the roads and tracks they use.

Some cargo travels by water. Workers load it onto ships. The ships often travel across oceans. Some ships carry many huge boxes. They hold food or other items. Other ships carry fuel.

Chapter 3

Carrying People

Many workers help people get around. Some workers drive **taxis**. Some are **rideshare** drivers. Others help people buy, fix, or rent cars.

Mass transit gives rides to many people at once. It includes buses and trains. Workers drive them. Some make many stops in one city. Others give longer rides. They go between cities.

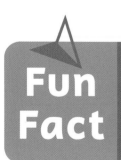

Engineers

Engineers are people who **design** things. Some work on new tunnels and bridges. Others design better roads. Engineers plan how to build these things. They choose what materials to use. They also check finished projects. They make sure each one stays safe and strong.

Chapter 4

Air Travel

Many people work at airports.
Some workers make sure
the planes are safe. Some
workers fix the planes. Others
help during flights. Pilots
fly the planes. The crew
helps **passengers**.

Some workers make **schedules** and plans. They help plan each plane's route. They make changes if there is bad weather. They also give **instructions** to pilots.

Fun Fact

Security workers help keep airports safe. They make sure no one brings dangerous items inside planes.

FOCUS ON
Transportation Workers

Write your answers on a separate piece of paper.

1. Write a sentence describing one job at an airport.

2. What is your favorite way to travel? What do you like about it?

3. Which job would an engineer do?
   - A. fly an airplane
   - B. drive a taxi
   - C. design a new bridge

4. What might happen if workers didn't plan each airplane's route?
   - A. Airplanes might crash into one another.
   - B. Airplanes might fly faster.
   - C. Airplanes might cost more to ride.

Answer key on page 24.

Glossary

cargo
Items carried by a vehicle from one place to another.

design
To plan how something will look or be made.

instructions
Steps that tell someone what to do.

passengers
People who ride in vehicles.

rideshare
A company that uses an app to match passengers with drivers.

routes
Ways of getting from one place to another.

schedules
Plans for what should happen and when it will take place.

taxis
Cars that people pay to ride in.

vehicles
Machines that carry things from place to place. Boats, trucks, trains, and airplanes are some examples.

To Learn More

BOOKS

Gaertner, Meg. *Delivery Drivers*. Minneapolis: Abdo Publishing, 2019.

Meinking, Mary. *Pilots*. North Mankato, MN: Capstone Publishing, 2020.

NOTE TO EDUCATORS

Visit **www.focusreaders.com** to find lesson plans, activities, links, and other resources related to this title.

Index

Answer Key: **1.** Answers will vary; **2.** Answers will vary; **3.** C; **4.** A